STATES OF MIND

I FEEL JEALOUS

BY STEPHANIE FINNE

TIPS FOR CAREGIVERS

Social and emotional learning (SEL) helps children manage emotions, create and achieve goals, maintain relationships, learn how to feel empathy, and make good decisions. The SEL approach will help children establish positive habits in communication, cooperation, and decision-making. By incorporating SEL in early reading, children will be better equipped to build confidence and foster positive peer networks.

BEFORE READING

Talk to the reader about how jealousy feels.

Discuss: How does your body feel when you are jealous? What kind of thoughts do you have?

AFTER READING

Talk to the reader about managing jealous feelings.

Discuss: What makes you feel jealous? What does this feeling tell you? How can you deal with it in a healthy way?

SEL GOAL

Some students may struggle with jealousy because they have a hard time with self-regulation. They may not be able to successfully consider their safety, respect for others, and appropriate social norms. Help them learn to pause and think about their actions. How can they identify their options? What do they need to do to control their impulses? Discuss how learning to do these things can help them manage feelings of jealousy and build positive relationships.

TABLE OF CONTENTS

CHAPTER 1
Jealousy and Envy 4

CHAPTER 2
Why So Jealous? 10

CHAPTER 3
How to Stop Feeling Jealous 16

GOALS AND TOOLS
Grow with Goals 22
Try This! 22
Glossary 23
To Learn More 23
Index 24

CHAPTER 1

JEALOUSY AND ENVY

Do you get upset when your best friend spends time with others? How about when your sibling is getting a lot of attention? This feeling is **jealousy**.

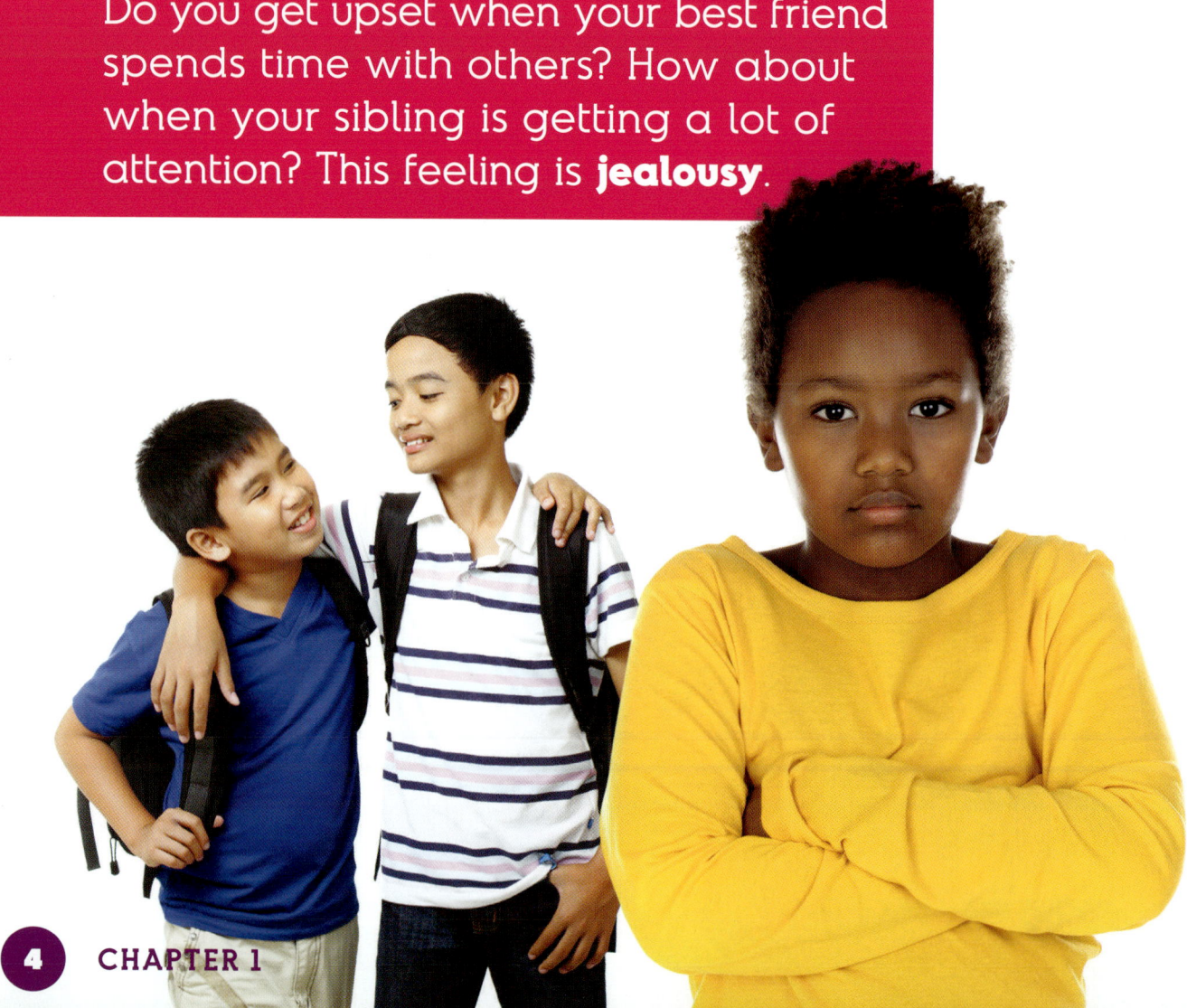

Jealousy happens when you feel like you are losing something. This **mood** can make you feel **possessive**. It can make you angry, too.

CHAPTER 1   5

CHAPTER 1

People use the words jealousy and **envy** to mean the same thing. But these moods are different. How? Envy is wanting something you don't have.

Cara's classmate has the best of everything. Cara's family can't afford expensive clothes and shoes. When she sees what she can't have, she feels envious.

CHAPTER 1   7

Jealousy and envy can feel similar. When you are jealous, your heart may race. Your stomach may get upset. Envy can make your cheeks hot and your body shake.

Kit's parents are busy with her baby brother. She gets jealous. She worries that they don't love her as much anymore. Her heart speeds up, and she gets angry.

GREEN-EYED MONSTER

Jealousy is often called "the green-eyed monster." Why? It feels like a monster you can't control is inside you.

CHAPTER 2
WHY SO JEALOUS?

Being jealous doesn't show love and caring. It means you feel **insecure** in your **relationships**. Why? You are afraid of losing someone.

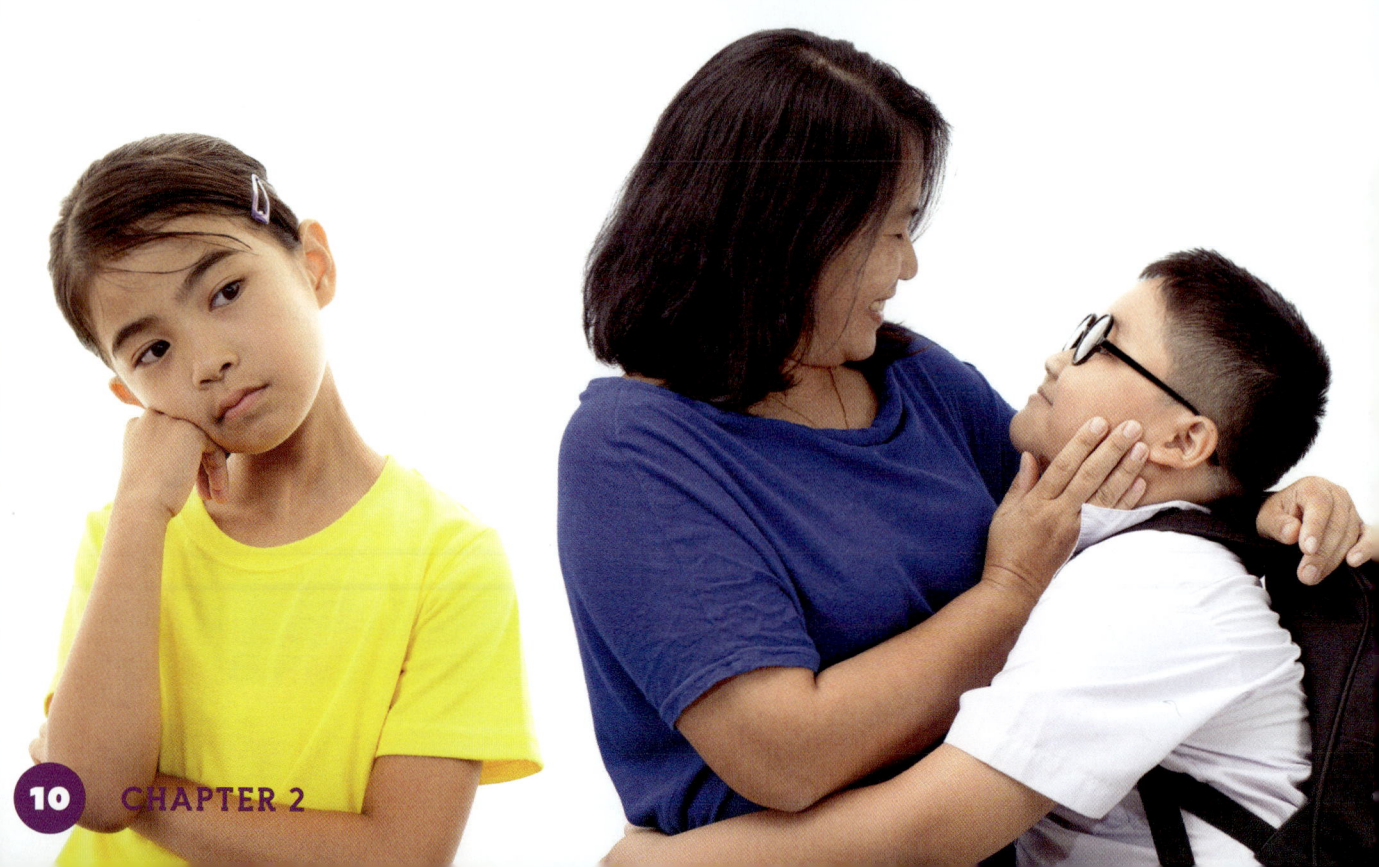

Envy happens when you **compare** yourself to someone. You measure your **self-worth** against what others have or can do. Sam feels envy when his cousin gets a video game he wants.

CHAPTER 2 | 11

CHAPTER 2

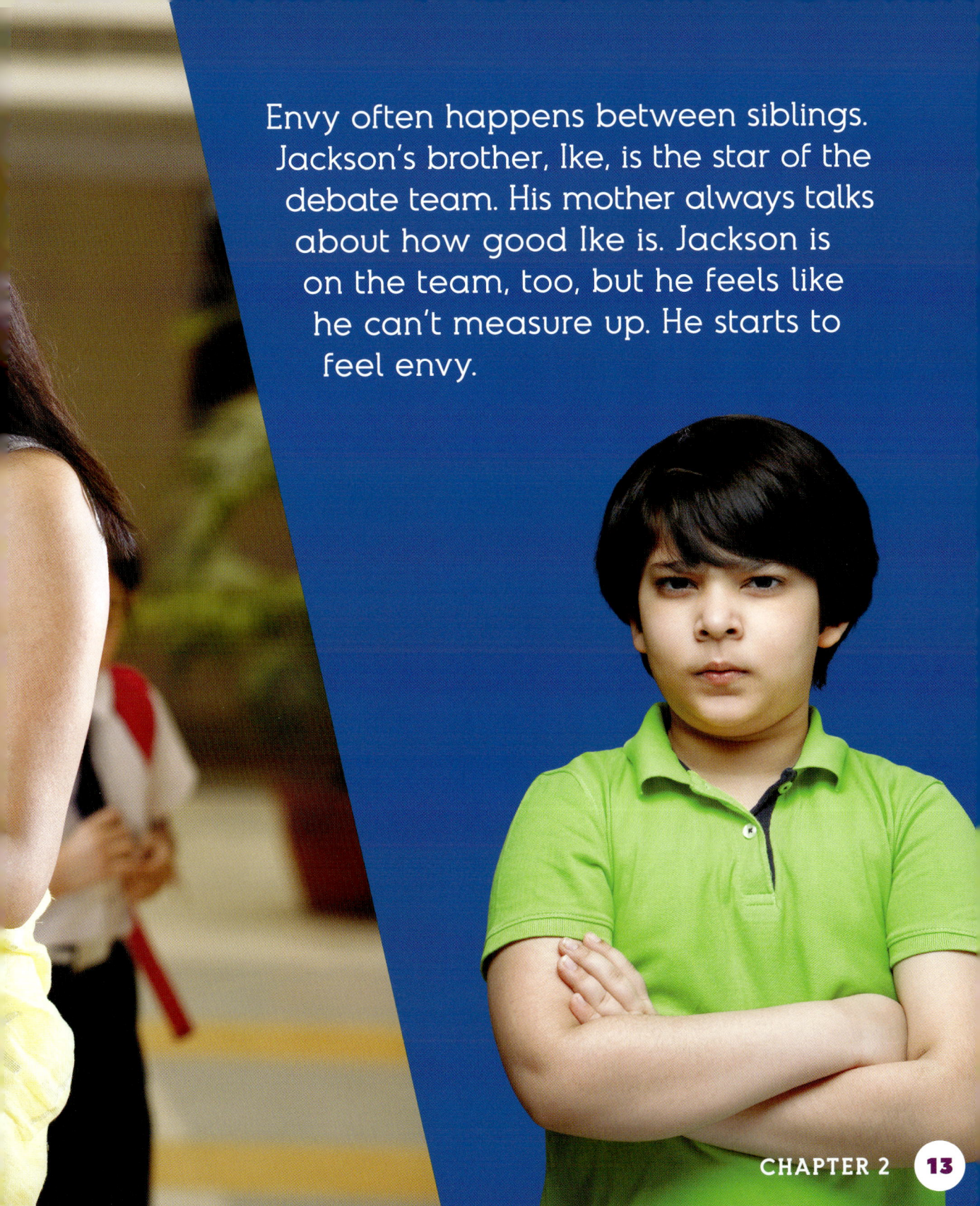

Envy often happens between siblings. Jackson's brother, Ike, is the star of the debate team. His mother always talks about how good Ike is. Jackson is on the team, too, but he feels like he can't measure up. He starts to feel envy.

CHAPTER 2   13

The fear of losing a friend can cause jealousy. It can be difficult to share close friends with others.

Molly's best friend, Lauren, went to a party without her. Molly feels left out. She worries that Lauren will become best friends with someone else. She feels possessive.

SOCIAL MEDIA

Social media can cause **stress** in friendships. How? It allows you to see what people are doing without you. Instead of checking online, find something else to do. You could exercise, create art, or volunteer your time.

CHAPTER 2

CHAPTER 3

HOW TO STOP FEELING JEALOUS

Jealousy hurts. It tells you that a relationship is in danger. Envy is difficult, too. It is tough to examine your self-worth. There are ways to stop these feelings.

First, be **mindful** of your feelings. What are they? How do they feel in your body? What do you think is causing them? Start a journal. Write your answers to these questions.

CHAPTER 3

Next, talk about your feelings. Being honest is not easy. But it can help you work through your feelings. If you can't talk to the person you are jealous or envious of, talk to another person you trust.

NEGATIVE SELF-TALK

Feeling jealous may lead to **negative self-talk**. If you tell yourself you aren't **worthy** of love, stop. Turn the negative to positive. Repeat "I am worthy."

CHAPTER 3   19

Finally, practice **gratitude**. Write down things you are grateful for. Then, make a list of **goals** for your relationships. Draw a picture or write about what you want to change. Work on these goals every day.

Be mindful of your feelings. Be honest with yourself and your loved ones. This will help you build healthy relationships!

CHAPTER 3

GOALS AND TOOLS

GROW WITH GOALS

Everyone feels jealous at times. Try these things to manage jealousy.

Goal: Be honest about your feelings. Identify your mood and what you think caused it.

Goal: Talk to a trusted adult about your feelings. Make a plan for how to improve the relationship that is causing jealousy.

Goal: Make a list of positive things about yourself. Remember that you are worthy of love and healthy relationships.

TRY THIS!

Start a gratitude journal. Gratitude is finding joy in the things you have. They can be possessions, skills, or relationships. This can help you see your talents and strengths. Every week, write down three things you are grateful for. Some examples could be your family or getting a good grade on a test. Write why you are grateful for these things and what your life would be like without them. Seeing the good in your life can help you feel less jealous.

GLOSSARY

compare
To judge one thing in relation to another in order to see the similarities and differences.

envy
A feeling of wanting what someone else has.

goals
Things you aim to do.

gratitude
A feeling of being grateful or thankful.

insecure
Not confident or sure of oneself.

jealousy
A feeling of fear that a person you love cares more for someone else than for you.

mindful
A mentality achieved by focusing on the present moment and calmly recognizing and accepting your feelings, thoughts, and sensations.

mood
An emotion that lasts longer than a few minutes.

negative self-talk
Words or thoughts to yourself that cause you to doubt yourself or your abilities and that limit your ability to believe in yourself.

possessive
Unwilling to share something or someone.

relationships
The ways in which people feel about and behave toward one another, or the ways in which two or more people are connected.

self-worth
One's own value as a human being.

stress
Mental or emotional strain or pressure.

worthy
Good enough and deserving of something.

TO LEARN MORE

Finding more information is as easy as 1, 2, 3.

1. Go to www.factsurfer.com
2. Enter "**Ifeeljealous**" into the search box.
3. Choose your book to see a list of websites.

INDEX

afraid 10

angry 5, 8

body 8, 17

compare 11

envy 7, 8, 11, 13, 16, 19

exercise 14

fear 14

friend 4, 14

goals 20

gratitude 20

honest 19, 20

insecure 10

losing 5, 10, 14

love 8, 10, 19

mindful 17, 20

mood 5, 7

negative self-talk 19

possessive 5, 14

relationships 10, 16, 20

self-worth 11, 16

sibling 4, 13

social media 14

stress 14

volunteer 14

worries 8, 14

write 17, 20

Blue Owl Books are published by Jump!, 5357 Penn Avenue South, Minneapolis, MN 55419, www.jumplibrary.com

Copyright © 2022 Jump! International copyright reserved in all countries. No part of this book may be reproduced in any form without written permission from the publisher.

Library of Congress Cataloging-in-Publication Data
Names: Finne, Stephanie, author.
Title: I feel jealous / by Stephanie Finne.
Description: Minneapolis, MN: Jump!, Inc., [2022]
Series: States of mind | Includes index. | Audience: Ages 7–10
Identifiers: LCCN 2020051046 (print)
LCCN 2020051047 (ebook)
ISBN 9781636901084 (hardcover)
ISBN 9781636901091 (paperback)
ISBN 9781636901107 (ebook)
Subjects: LCSH: Jealousy in children—Juvenile literature. | Jealousy—Juvenile literature.
Classification: LCC BF723.J4 F56 2022 (print) | LCC BF723.J4 (ebook) | DDC 155.4/1248–dc23
LC record available at https://lccn.loc.gov/2020051046
LC ebook record available at https://lccn.loc.gov/2020051047

Editor: Eliza Leahy
Designer: Michelle Sonnek

Photo Credits: Laboo Studio/Shutterstock, cover (left); Rawpixel.com/Shutterstock, cover (right); Anurak Pongpatimet/Shutterstock, 1 (left); YinYang/iStock, 1 (right); sirikorn thamniyom/Shutterstock, 3 (left); New Africa/Shutterstock, 3 (right); pedalist/Shutterstock, 4 (left); Gelpi/Shutterstock, 4 (right); ViDI Studio/Shutterstock, 5; SDI Productions/iStock, 6–7; 5 second Studio/Shutterstock, 7; Tatyana Dzemileva/Shutterstock, 8–9; sunabesyou/Shutterstock, 10 (left); kwanchai.c/Shutterstock, 10 (right); Marcel Mooij/Shutterstock, 11; triloks/iStock, 12–13, 17; Deepak Sethi/iStock, 13; Pressmaster/Shutterstock, 14–15; vystekimages/Shutterstock, 16; Syda Productions/Shutterstock, 18–19; gradyreese/iStock, 20–21.

Printed in the United States of America at Corporate Graphics in North Mankato, Minnesota.

24 GOALS AND TOOLS